The ★ UNITED STATES PRESIDENTS

★ ★ Martin ★ ★

VAN BUREN

BreAnn Rumsch

Big Buddy Books

An Imprint of Abdo Publishing
abdopublishing.com

abdopublishing.com

Published by Abdo Publishing, a division of ABDO, PO Box 398166, Minneapolis, Minnesota 55439. Copyright © 2017 by Abdo Consulting Group, Inc. International copyrights reserved in all countries. No part of this book may be reproduced in any form without written permission from the publisher. Big Buddy Books™ is a trademark and logo of Abdo Publishing.

Printed in the United States of America, North Mankato, Minnesota
062016
092016

THIS BOOK CONTAINS
RECYCLED MATERIALS

Design: Sarah DeYoung, Mighty Media, Inc.
Production: Mighty Media, Inc.
Editor: Rebecca Felix
Cover Photograph: Getty Images
Interior Photographs: Alamy (p. 27); Corbis (pp. 11, 13, 29); Library of Congress (pp. 5, 6, 7, 9, 15, 17, 19, 25); Picture History (pp. 21, 23)

Cataloging-in-Publication Data

Names: Rumsch, BreAnn., author.
Title: Martin Van Buren / by BreAnn Rumsch.
Description: Minneapolis, MN : Abdo Publishing, [2017] | Series: United States presidents | Includes bibliographical references and index.
Identifiers: LCCN 2015957561 | ISBN 9781680781212 (lib. bdg.) | ISBN 9781680775419 (ebook)
Subjects: LCSH: Van Buren, Martin, 1782-1862--Juvenile literature. | Presidents--United States--Biography--Juvenile literature. | United States--Politics and government--1837-1841--Juvenile literature.
Classification: DDC 973.5/7092 [B]--dc23
LC record available at http://lccn.loc.gov/2015957561

Contents

Martin Van Buren

Martin Van Buren was the eighth US president. He served in many public offices. Van Buren was a New York state senator and a US senator. He was also governor of New York.

In 1829, Van Buren became **secretary of state**. He became vice president in 1833. Three years later, Van Buren became president.

Van Buren is best remembered for two things. He founded America's first **political machine**. He also organized the **Democratic** Party.

Timeline

1782

On December 5, Martin Van Buren was born in Kinderhook, New York.

1821

Van Buren was elected to the US Senate.

1812

Van Buren was elected to the New York senate.

1828

Van Buren was elected governor of New York.

1833

Van Buren became US vice president.

1829

President Andrew Jackson named Van Buren **secretary of state**.

1837

In March, Van Buren became the eighth US president.

1862

On July 24, Martin Van Buren died.

Kinderhook Youth

Martin Van Buren was born in Kinderhook, New York, on December 5, 1782. His parents were named Maria and Abraham.

Martin was the third of Abraham and Maria's five children. He also had two half brothers. He had one half sister.

★ FAST FACTS ★

Born: December 5, 1782

Wife: Hannah Hoes (1783–1819)

Children: four

Political Party: Democrat

Age at Inauguration: 54

Years Served: 1837–1841

Vice President: Richard M. Johnson

Died: July 24, 1862, age 79

Martin's birthplace was also the site of his father's tavern. Today, all that remains is a historical marker.

Learning the Law

In 1796, Van Buren became a law clerk. He worked for a **lawyer** named Francis Silvester. In 1801, Van Buren traveled to New York City. There, he completed his law studies.

Van Buren passed his law test in 1803. He became a lawyer. He joined his half brother James Van Alen at a law office in Kinderhook.

On February 21, 1807, Van Buren married Hannah Hoes. The couple had four sons. Van Buren raised his sons alone after his wife died in February 1819.

Hannah Van Buren
and her husband
named their four sons
Abraham, John,
Martin Jr.,
and Smith.

New York Leader

In 1808, Van Buren got his first job in **politics**. He became **surrogate** of Columbia County, New York. Van Buren was elected to the New York senate in 1812.

In 1816, Van Buren was reelected state senator. That year, he **supported** a bill to build the Erie **Canal**. It would improve **transportation** and business in New York.

Also in 1816, Van Buren became **attorney general**. He remained as state senator. Van Buren held both positions for several years.

The Erie Canal connects New York City to the Great Lakes by way of the Hudson River. It was completed in 1825.

Political Machine

While serving as New York senator, Van Buren led a group of **Democratic-Republicans**. They were called the bucktails. Van Buren helped put party **supporters** in state government jobs.

As more and more bucktails were hired, the Democratic-Republican Party's power grew. Soon, Van Buren's supporters formed a **political machine**. In 1821, they chose Van Buren to run for the US Senate. He won the election! Van Buren was off to Washington, DC.

Van Buren's political machine lasted for nearly 30 years.

To the Capitol

Van Buren was a US senator from 1821 to 1828. He was elected governor of New York in 1828. But he would not remain there long.

In March 1829, Andrew Jackson became president. He made Van Buren his **secretary of state**. So, Van Buren left the governorship.

As secretary of state, Van Buren made **treaties** with other countries. In 1830, Turkey agreed to allow US ships in the Black Sea. That same year, Great Britain agreed to allow the United States to trade in the West Indies.

Andrew Jackson
was president from
1829 to 1837.

In 1831, Van Buren left his position as **secretary of state**. Meanwhile, the **Democratic-Republican** Party had split in two. Van Buren and others formed what became known as the **Democratic** Party.

In 1832, President Jackson was up for reelection. The Democrats chose Van Buren as his **running mate**. Jackson won. So, Van Buren became vice president on March 4, 1833.

In 1836, Van Buren ran for president. He won. However, no person running for vice president won a majority of the votes. So, the US Senate chose the winner. It chose Kentucky **representative** Richard M. Johnson.

Before becoming vice president, Richard M. Johnson served in the US House of Representatives and the US Senate.

President Van Buren

Van Buren became president in March 1837. Soon after, the Panic of 1837 began. It was the first great **depression** in US history. Van Buren believed some banks were to blame. He felt they had not used government money carefully.

Van Buren asked Congress to form an independent **treasury**. It would control which banks had permission to use government money. Van Buren felt this would prevent another depression. But Congress voted against forming the treasury.

Angelica Singleton Van Buren was Van Buren's daughter-in-law. She served as White House hostess during his presidency.

In late 1837, Van Buren faced problems with Canada. The Canadians wanted independence from Great Britain. Some Americans wanted to help the Canadians. But Van Buren said America would not take sides.

At the same time, US troops were fighting Seminole Native Americans in Florida. White Americans wanted the tribe's land there. The **Second Seminole War** lasted from 1835 to 1842. Thousands of people died in battle.

Meanwhile, President Van Buren continued to fight Congress for an independent **treasury**. On July 4, 1840, Congress finally passed the Independent Treasury Act.

The independent
treasury bill.
Van Buren called
this document a
"second declaration
of independence."

Also in 1840, Van Buren ran for reelection. The **Democrats** could not agree on who to choose to run for vice president. So, Van Buren ran without a **running mate**. He became the only president in US history to do so.

However, some of the events during Van Buren's presidency had made him unpopular. This cost him many votes. So, Van Buren lost the election.

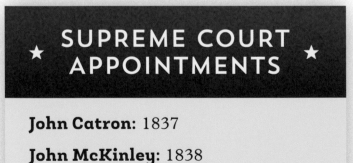

SUPREME COURT APPOINTMENTS

John Catron: 1837

John McKinley: 1838

Peter V. Daniel: 1842

PRESIDENT VAN BUREN'S CABINET

March 4, 1837–March 4, 1841

★ **STATE:** John Forsyth

★ **TREASURY:** Levi Woodbury

★ **WAR:** Joel Roberts Poinsett

★ **NAVY:** Mahlon Dickerson,
James Kirke Paulding
(from July 1, 1838)

★ **ATTORNEY GENERAL:**
Benjamin Franklin Butler,
Felix Grundy (from September 1, 1838),
Henry Dilworth Gilpin
(from January 11, 1840)

Lifelong Politician

Van Buren left the White House in March 1841. He moved to Lindenwald. This was his country home in Kinderhook. However, Van Buren continued to work in **politics**.

In 1844, Van Buren decided to run for president again. But some of his views made him unpopular. So, he was not chosen to run.

The next year, the United States **annexed** Texas. This caused the **Democratic** Party to split into two groups. They were known as the hunkers and the barnburners.

Van Buren named his estate
Lindenwald after the many
linden trees on the property.

Van Buren led the barnburners. They wanted to stop slavery from spreading. In 1848, the barnburners chose Van Buren to run for president. But Van Buren's views against slavery upset many Americans. So, he lost the election.

In the following years, Van Buren traveled around Europe. He returned to Kinderhook in 1855. On July 24, 1862, Van Buren died at Lindenwald.

Martin Van Buren faced many challenges during his presidency. He also made important changes to **politics**. He helped organize the **Democratic** Party and **supported** it throughout his life.

In the 1848 election, Charles Francis Adams ran as Van Buren's vice president.

Office of the President

Branches of Government

The US government has three branches. They are the executive, legislative, and judicial branches. Each branch has some power over the others. This is called a system of checks and balances.

★ Executive Branch

The executive branch enforces laws. It is made up of the president, the vice president, and the president's cabinet. The president represents the United States around the world. He or she also signs bills into law and leads the military.

★ Legislative Branch

The legislative branch makes laws, maintains the military, and regulates trade. It also has the power to declare war. This branch includes the Senate and the House of Representatives. Together, these two houses form Congress.

★ Judicial Branch

The judicial branch interprets laws. It is made up of district courts, courts of appeals, and the Supreme Court. District courts try cases. Sometimes people disagree with a trial's outcome. Then he or she may appeal. If a court of appeals supports the ruling, a person may appeal to the Supreme Court.

Qualifications for Office

To be president, a candidate must be at least 35 years old. The person must be a natural-born US citizen. He or she must also have lived in the United States for at least 14 years.

Electoral College

The US presidential election is an indirect election. Voters from each state choose electors. These electors represent their state in the Electoral College. Each elector has one electoral vote. Electors cast their vote for the candidate with the highest number of votes from people in their state. A candidate must receive the majority of Electoral College votes to win.

Term of Office

Each president may be elected to two four-year terms. The presidential election is held on the Tuesday after the first Monday in November. The president is sworn in on January 20 of the following year. At that time, he or she takes the oath of office.
It states:

> I do solemnly swear (or affirm) that I will faithfully execute the office of President of the United States, and will to the best of my ability, preserve, protect and defend the Constitution of the United States.

31

Line of Succession

The Presidential Succession Act of 1947 states who becomes president if the president cannot serve. The vice president is first in the line. Next are the Speaker of the House and the President Pro Tempore of the Senate. It may happen that none of these individuals is able to serve. Then the office falls to the president's cabinet members. They would take office in the order in which each department was created:

Secretary of State

Secretary of the Treasury

Secretary of Defense

Attorney General

Secretary of the Interior

Secretary of Agriculture

Secretary of Commerce

Secretary of Labor

Secretary of Health and Human Services

Secretary of Housing and Urban Development

Secretary of Transportation

Secretary of Energy

Secretary of Education

Secretary of Veterans Affairs

Secretary of Homeland Security

Benefits

★ While in office, the president receives a salary. It is $400,000 per year. He or she lives in the White House. The president also has 24-hour Secret Service protection.

★ The president may travel on a Boeing 747 jet. This special jet is called Air Force One. It can hold 70 passengers. It has kitchens, a dining room, sleeping areas, and more. Air Force One can fly halfway around the world before needing to refuel. It can even refuel in flight!

★ When the president travels by car, he or she uses Cadillac One. It is a Cadillac Deville that has been modified. The car has heavy armor and communications systems. The president may even take Cadillac One along when visiting other countries.

★ The president also travels on a helicopter. It is called Marine One. It may also be taken along when the president visits other countries.

★ Sometimes the president needs to get away with family and friends. Camp David is the official presidential retreat. It is located in Maryland. The US Navy maintains the retreat. The US Marine Corps keeps it secure. The camp offers swimming, tennis, golf, and hiking.

★ When the president leaves office, he or she receives lifetime Secret Service protection. He or she also receives a yearly pension of $203,700. The former president also receives money for office space, supplies, and staff.

PRESIDENTS AND THEIR TERMS

PRESIDENT	PARTY	TOOK OFFICE	LEFT OFFICE	TERMS SERVED	VICE PRESIDENT
George Washington	None	April 30, 1789	March 4, 1797	Two	John Adams
John Adams	Federalist	March 4, 1797	March 4, 1801	One	Thomas Jefferson
Thomas Jefferson	Democratic-Republican	March 4, 1801	March 4, 1809	Two	Aaron Burr, George Clinton
James Madison	Democratic-Republican	March 4, 1809	March 4, 1817	Two	George Clinton, Elbridge Gerry
James Monroe	Democratic-Republican	March 4, 1817	March 4, 1825	Two	Daniel D. Tompkins
John Quincy Adams	Democratic-Republican	March 4, 1825	March 4, 1829	One	John C. Calhoun
Andrew Jackson	Democrat	March 4, 1829	March 4, 1837	Two	John C. Calhoun, Martin Van Buren
Martin Van Buren	Democrat	March 4, 1837	March 4, 1841	One	Richard M. Johnson
William H. Harrison	Whig	March 4, 1841	April 4, 1841	Died During First Term	John Tyler
John Tyler	Whig	April 6, 1841	March 4, 1845	Completed Harrison's Term	Office Vacant
James K. Polk	Democrat	March 4, 1845	March 4, 1849	One	George M. Dallas
Zachary Taylor	Whig	March 5, 1849	July 9, 1850	Died During First Term	Millard Fillmore

PRESIDENT	PARTY	TOOK OFFICE	LEFT OFFICE	TERMS SERVED	VICE PRESIDENT
Millard Fillmore	Whig	July 10, 1850	March 4, 1853	Completed Taylor's Term	Office Vacant
Franklin Pierce	Democrat	March 4, 1853	March 4, 1857	One	William R.D. King
James Buchanan	Democrat	March 4, 1857	March 4, 1861	One	John C. Breckinridge
Abraham Lincoln	Republican	March 4, 1861	April 15, 1865	Served One Term, Died During Second Term	Hannibal Hamlin, Andrew Johnson
Andrew Johnson	Democrat	April 15, 1865	March 4, 1869	Completed Lincoln's Second Term	Office Vacant
Ulysses S. Grant	Republican	March 4, 1869	March 4, 1877	Two	Schuyler Colfax, Henry Wilson
Rutherford B. Hayes	Republican	March 3, 1877	March 4, 1881	One	William A. Wheeler
James A. Garfield	Republican	March 4, 1881	September 19, 1881	Died During First Term	Chester Arthur
Chester Arthur	Republican	September 20, 1881	March 4, 1885	Completed Garfield's Term	Office Vacant
Grover Cleveland	Democrat	March 4, 1885	March 4, 1889	One	Thomas A. Hendricks
Benjamin Harrison	Republican	March 4, 1889	March 4, 1893	One	Levi P. Morton
Grover Cleveland	Democrat	March 4, 1893	March 4, 1897	One	Adlai E. Stevenson
William McKinley	Republican	March 4, 1897	September 14, 1901	Served One Term, Died During Second Term	Garret A. Hobart, Theodore Roosevelt

PRESIDENT	PARTY	TOOK OFFICE	LEFT OFFICE	TERMS SERVED	VICE PRESIDENT
Theodore Roosevelt	Republican	September 14, 1901	March 4, 1909	Completed McKinley's Second Term, Served One Term	Office Vacant, Charles Fairbanks
William Taft	Republican	March 4, 1909	March 4, 1913	One	James S. Sherman
Woodrow Wilson	Democrat	March 4, 1913	March 4, 1921	Two	Thomas R. Marshall
Warren G. Harding	Republican	March 4, 1921	August 2, 1923	Died During First Term	Calvin Coolidge
Calvin Coolidge	Republican	August 3, 1923	March 4, 1929	Completed Harding's Term, Served One Term	Office Vacant, Charles Dawes
Herbert Hoover	Republican	March 4, 1929	March 4, 1933	One	Charles Curtis
Franklin D. Roosevelt	Democrat	March 4, 1933	April 12, 1945	Served Three Terms, Died During Fourth Term	John Nance Garner, Henry A. Wallace, Harry S. Truman
Harry S. Truman	Democrat	April 12, 1945	January 20, 1953	Completed Roosevelt's Fourth Term, Served One Term	Office Vacant, Alben Barkley
Dwight D. Eisenhower	Republican	January 20, 1953	January 20, 1961	Two	Richard Nixon
John F. Kennedy	Democrat	January 20, 1961	November 22, 1963	Died During First Term	Lyndon B. Johnson
Lyndon B. Johnson	Democrat	November 22, 1963	January 20, 1969	Completed Kennedy's Term, Served One Term	Office Vacant, Hubert H. Humphrey
Richard Nixon	Republican	January 20, 1969	August 9, 1974	Completed First Term, Resigned During Second Term	Spiro T. Agnew, Gerald Ford

PRESIDENT	PARTY	TOOK OFFICE	LEFT OFFICE	TERMS SERVED	VICE PRESIDENT
Gerald Ford	Republican	August 9, 1974	January 20, 1977	Completed Nixon's Second Term	Nelson A. Rockefeller
Jimmy Carter	Democrat	January 20, 1977	January 20, 1981	One	Walter Mondale
Ronald Reagan	Republican	January 20, 1981	January 20, 1989	Two	George H.W. Bush
George H.W. Bush	Republican	January 20, 1989	January 20, 1993	One	Dan Quayle
Bill Clinton	Democrat	January 20, 1993	January 20, 2001	Two	Al Gore
George W. Bush	Republican	January 20, 2001	January 20, 2009	Two	Dick Cheney
Barack Obama	Democrat	January 20, 2009	January 20, 2017	Two	Joe Biden

"**The less government interferes, the better for general prosperity.**" Martin Van Buren

★ WRITE TO THE PRESIDENT ★

You may write to the president at:
The White House
1600 Pennsylvania Avenue NW
Washington, DC 20500

You may e-mail the president at:
comments@whitehouse.gov

37

Glossary

annex—to take land and add it to a nation.

attorney general—the chief lawyer of a country or state who represents the government in legal matters.

canal—a channel dug across land to connect two bodies of water so ships can pass through.

Democrat—a member of the Democratic political party.

Democratic-Republican—a member of the Democratic-Republican political party.

depression—a period of economic trouble when there is little buying or selling and many people are out of work.

lawyer (LAW-yuhr)—a person who gives people advice on laws or represents them in court.

political machine—a highly organized political group under the leadership of a boss.

politics—the art or science of government. Something referring to politics is political. A person who is active in politics is a politician.

representative—someone chosen in an election to act or speak for the people who voted for him or her.

running mate—someone running for vice president with another person running for president in an election.

Second Seminole War—from 1835 to 1842. A battle between the Seminole Native Americans and the US government to remove the Seminole from their Florida lands.

secretary of state—a member of the president's cabinet who handles relations with other countries.

support—to believe in or be in favor of something.

surrogate—a court officer in some states who handles the settling of wills.

transportation—the act of moving people or things from one place to another.

treasury—a place where money is kept.

treaty—an agreement made between two or more groups.

★ WEBSITES ★

To learn more about the US Presidents, visit **booklinks.abdopublishing.com**. These links are routinely monitored and updated to provide the most current information available.

Index